PRAISE FOR TAISIA KITAISKAIA

"For fans of Taisia Kitaiskaia's previous books, I'm here to tell you her poetry debut is every bit as wild, witchy, and visionary as you could have hoped. In *The Nightgown*, Taisia's ongoing exploration of the folklore of the self voyages into exciting new territory. Prepare to step inside a menagerie of evil potatoes and misbehaving angels, imaginary gardens and real toads. It's an experience as beguiling as a wedding ceremony you never fully learn the rules to. This book left me completely drunk and I don't regret it and neither will you."

—Dobby Gibson, *Little Glass Planet*

"What do you expect to see w　　　　　　 deeply into the foreign wounds on your body? Taisia s　　　　　　　　　　　ie tender bog, how to relish the unki　　　　　　　　　　　 and . . . Please, don't be alarmed whe　　　　　　　　　　　 draw a card that speaks too loud. It i　　　　　　　　　　　 waiting for you to break the ice."

—Jiyoon Lee, *Foreigner's Folly*

"Fairytales are grim creatures, part teeth, part terror, but nevertheless, too seductive to resist. Taisia's poems 'crawl out from the river' like a nymph, to offer that poisoned apple, of which I gladly bite, in search of 'that imaginary orgasm.'"

—mónica teresa ortiz, *muted blood*

"*The Nightgown* is not the ethereal, diaphanous sleeping frock of fairytales. It's carnal, fleshly. Its angels have hairy fingers. A soul is a thing you can pet. There's lots of butter, meat, glasses of milk. The love is strenuous, and the impossible starves on. The only thing these poems have in common with fairytales is their dark brain and crepuscular faces. I'm ensorcelled by their logic, which is soluble in its own sentences (and the syllogisms are such: if you're ravished by a rabbit, you've been rabbished, haha). The poems read like stories, but they are not going forward to an end—they are going backward, into the history of their own words. In one poem, the writer asks if she can be a man of God and the poem ends 'the little wormings, I do love'—ahh, yes!—not the book she is writing, or the words, but the insects that eat them, which, of course, in these poems of Anglo-Saxon meatiness are called wormings. I loved the words in these poems. Where oh where, Taisia Kitaiskaia, did you get those nouns!? What big texture you have! It would be perfect if this book's cover were made of human hair, and we could stroke it as we read."

—Darcie Dennigan, *Palace of Subatomic Bliss*

"Taisia's poems make you think of the poem as an apothecary's pill . . . without being able to verify its true origins, and getting only some encrypted apothecary verse that provides only the faintest suggestion of what elements the pill might even contain, you take it anyway, you trust it almost completely . . . a pill presented ever neatly, yet ominously, to you in the palm of your hand, a pill that appears to encapsulate an entire psychosomatic experience. Taisia's fablesque poems come from this far-away place, or, rather, a place we are made to believe is faraway but is really just close enough to have heard enough news of civilization's operas. To read these poems, we must walk along a trail that moves from idyllic to horrific and then back again in the pace of a gallop before we reach the door to the apothecary who will gift us that pill, equal parts restorative and poison. It is this tension between that which is presented tenderly and that which menacingly refuses total encapsulation, which makes the most lanuginous of us curl up at the base of the rocking chair and ask the storyteller for 'another one!' again and again.

—Valerie Hsiung, *You & Me Forever*

The Nightgown
and Other Poems

Taisia Kitaiskaia

DEEP VELLUM PUBLISHING

DALLAS, TEXAS

Deep Vellum Publishing
3000 Commerce St., Dallas, Texas 75226
deepvellum.org · @deepvellum

Deep Vellum is a 501c3 nonprofit literary arts organization
founded in 2013 with the mission to bring
the world into conversation through literature.

Support for this publication has been provided in part by grants from the
National Endowment for the Arts, the Texas Commission on the Arts, the City
of Dallas Office of Arts and Culture's ArtsActivate program, and the Moody
Fund for the Arts:

ISBNs: 978-1-64605-027-7 (paperback) | 978-1-64605-028-4 (ebook)

LIBRARY OF CONGRESS CATALOGING IN PUBLICATION DATA

Names: Kitaiskaia, Taisia, author.
Title: The nightgown : and other poems / Taisia Kitaiskaia.
Description: First edition. | Dallas, Texas : Deep Vellum Publishing, 2020.
Identifiers: LCCN 2020010250 (print) | LCCN 2020010251 (ebook) | ISBN
    9781646050277 (paperback) | ISBN 9781646050284 (ebook)
Subjects: LCGFT: Poetry.
Classification: LCC PS3611.I876 N54 2020 (print) | LCC PS3611.I876
    (ebook) | DDC 811/.6--dc23
LC record available at https://lccn.loc.gov/2020010250
LC ebook record available at https://lccn.loc.gov/2020010251

Cover Art and Design © 2020 by Emma Steinkraus
Interior Layout and Typesetting by Kirby Gann

Text set in Bembo, a typeface modeled on typefaces cut by Francesco Griffo
for Aldo Manuzio's printing of *De Aetna* in 1495 in Venice.

Printed in the United States of America

for my parents

CONTENTS

The Nightgown and Other Poems

THE FOLKLORE

Shortly after crawling from the river, the folklore
Died of pernicious diseases. Died upside down
In our wishing well, showing its bloomers.
Someone spat on the folklore. Someone dipped
The folklore, like a candle, in lye. Someone
Washed the folklore's corpse. Someone put
The folklore under a sun lamp, but the folklore
Did not revive. When I next saw the folklore,
It was filing papers in a basement office,
Trying to tip the vending machine over, loving
The salty and the sweet. I shook out all the snacks,
Now I am the ugly wife of the folklore, we kiss
Our ugly faces together, clammy. We go out
For ice cream, we love apples, we hold hands
Under the table. We eat peanuts, wipe grease
On our skirts, get married over and over. We
Are tipsy in the hot afternoon, swaying along
With the sunflowers. Once a year the folklore
Rides away on a little pig, I weep in our manor,
I shield my eyes with straw. Then the folklore
Comes back with beads, honeycombs, GigaPets,
We are in love again. Knocking against each other,
Lurking in each other's dreams like sharks.
We go to the natural history museum, disappear
Into the tanned cloaks of extinct peoples. We,
Too, are extinct and rolling down a hill, scooped
By grass. How much longer can we go on living,
Dying, seeking the other in each inherited world.
When you, the folklore, first swam towards me,
You grabbed my ankles, you heaved yourself
Onto the banks, onto me. Dripping, we began.

THE HURT OPERA

The opera kneels all night
In her desperate colors
On the kitchen floor.

Bruised, ancient opera.

Her inky sap drips down
Spring's fresh glass.

Like an insect, she can't
Be trained. The dentist says

Her fillings, made of tiny crushed
Flies, must be replaced: *She* says

That's how she likes them.
Dingy, mean opera.

When she makes me dinner,
There is no love between us,
Only eels,

Still alive in their butter
And anger. On walks,
The opera pulls cold turnips

Straight from the ground,
Watches my face as she bites,
As if to say, *Yes,*

I came from your raw
Dark pocket, but I shall live
Without you as a monk

Lives without water. Scary
Opera. Stingy, lean opera.

I am just a simple man.
I hold her head when it leaks,
And call out when she shrinks

Smaller than her name
In encyclopedia.

MY TIME WITH THE ANGELS

I climbed the beanstalk, up and up, to the realm
Of pendulous curtains. The angels hid, emerged
With grape jelly hands, long black hair, greening
Toenails. One angel relieved itself, glaring at me
Erstwhile. The angels stooped in the same linen
They'd worn for millennia, traveling over road-
Tongues that could retract at any moment, gather
The angels into balls; contraptions created, of course,
By the angels, who schemed with their abaci. When
Wanting love, the angels prodded each other with bristly
Sticks. They had one field with a children's kitchen,
Little plastic melons and bananas, plastic toast
With butter. Regularly an angel forayed, sat down
In a tiny chair and tried to halve a melon or spread
Butter as the other angels laughed, hooting, pointing,
The kitchen angel turning red under unwashed hair.
Nevertheless every angel in the community visited
The kitchen once a year, or such were my calculations.
The angels had a herd of shrubs, often missing; one
Was suicidal. The angels had a criminal odor, but
It was unclear if they had no laws or many. Nightly
They poured milk into a dirty glass and squatted
Around to watch me drink. The milk was repulsive—
It came from the shrubs' teats—but I was afraid of
The angels then, their grunting and burning. For years
After my time with the angels, I felt compelled to do
Things I loathed, like watch movies starring Cate
Blanchett, because the angels, living through me, knew
Cate to be a truer angel than they, and were ashamed.
In my extensive scholarship on angels, I argue
That shame and rebellion are integral to the angels,

But these publications were pressured by tenure,
I don't believe a word. Once I had drunk the milk,
An angel would always reach in and fish a black fly
From the glass bottom with a single hairy finger,
Either to save the creature for my next humiliation,
Or perhaps as an apology, I could never be sure.

MY EVIL TWIN

I feel nostalgic for my evil twin. He used
To lurk around my yard like a goblin,
Sticking his head into bags of leaves.
We worked for the government together,
That's how we met. Weird we didn't
Meet earlier, but the twin was like that.
He had a name like "Laredo" or "Marshall"
Or "Le Faz," I could never keep track.
He'd show up to Christmas and spit
In the pudding. He loved to blowdry
His tender bits at the dinner table.
(What was he doing to keep them so
Moist, breeding caterpillars?) I stopped
Inviting him, of course, but he followed
Me around like a moon-faced armadillo
Through heaps of light. Heaps! He liked
To carry marshmallows in his handbag
Like a typical child. He was in love
With me, that was the worst thing about it.
His love and my repulsion made a sewer
In which dolphins swam, growing grimmer
Daily until they stopped smiling altogether.
Plus, I was tired of the grind. Working
In an office, stapling memos to my back
Like an ancient Egyptian. Merciless,
Merciless! That's the world and its lashes,
Said the twin, and he got that much right.
But the twin only made things worse.
His pots and pans always gleaming
With clean urine, his toadstools ever ready
With unkind wisecracks. My twin, he

Disastered all over the place, tricking
Pretty baristas into going a-blimping
With him, and then lo-and-behold,
There he'd be, jumping blimp, leaving
The barista to fend for herself in the clouds.
I grew tireder and tireder, it was time
To do something. With great resignation,
I wrapped my twin up with twine and
Gifted him to a large, wealthy family
Who mistook him for a clever goose,
The kind that can nanny your children.
Fair enough. I wept then, not for him
But for the aimless struggle of my life,
The never-good-nor-badness of it,
Like a thick smear of paint over lips
Trying to eat a grape. Like lying in a
Ghost's belly and all the alarm clocks
Are going off, but the ghost doesn't
Give a damn. It's a miracle anyone
Has ever looked at you or drawn your
Profile on a napkin. I'm going to order
An entire cherry pie, and when the waitress
Kicks me out at half-past midnight,
I'll leak what remains of my spirit
Into this glass of milk, my criminal
Powder a poison that makes the waitress
Glow radioactive when she steals a sip,
And when we meet on the other side,
Maybe the twin can solve my murder.

HOUR OF MONKS

The monks drink their silence wine.
No one watches them.
They could fall asleep facedown in a hill
And no one would know.
I would like some butter with my bread.
I will eat dark bread and think about the lone monk
Lying facedown on a green hill.

A fox approaches him.
The fox sniffs.
I look away as the fox does the other things it will do.

The monk lies silent as bread.
The monk is terrible and small.

Whatever the monk believed, we believe him.
No one believes the fox.
No one believes my dark bread and glass of milk.
My house this morning is a green hill
And my bread is black, the color of earth and speed.
My eye is black and the house is black as bread.

The monk lies sleeping in the dead.
His monk brothers drink wine in silence.

I am small.
I am actually a child.
The silence has made humps in my shoulders.

Whatever the earth is,
It is much better to eat dark bread
And think on what it was.

It is enough to make the brain dark.

THE NIGHTGOWN

Rabbits have bitten holes in my nightgown,
Which have only made her more sensuous. I am
A sensuous housewife, candles everywhere are dying
To see me naked. But I'm never naked, there's always
A thick eye deep inside me, recording and reporting
To the other planets. I wear my nightgown in the daytime
Out of stubbornness and resentment. I unhinge elegant,
Fatal formulas in my notebooks; the nightgown glares
With her many heads. I watch my mystery novels, eat,
I peruse, I harbor sandwiches, I am lofty. My lovers
Waltz on my nightgown, we float on my nightgown's
Boat. One of my organs is a meaningless word,
Such as PARABOLA. It itched itself into my regions,
A boomerang in my lung branches, electric with grief.
This is a story about my nightgown, who is riding
The elevator. Your attentions to my nightgown have not
Gone unnoticed, but beware, she has a canid's loyalty
And jaws. Just yesterday she sat up on her hind legs
To frighten me. My malice rises daily, it will drench
The nightgown with black bile. Lovers bring flowers
To my nightgown and she is naïve, she believes everything.
She is plain as a pail, perhaps she has a secret dowry.
It is hard to imagine someone kissing the nightgown,
But the impossible starves on. Meanwhile I strive
In the corner over my formulas. My regions are aflame,
I've had to remove the PARABOLA with tweezers,
Place it on a saucer. The nightgown gobbled it instantly.
She is a monster, she should be locked up. She is fat
With PARABOLA. She winces as she walks. Her moods
Consume this house, spit it out as a TV programme
Called "My Troubles." I rarely see the nightgown anymore,

But still her anger rams into me with a thousand sturgeons.
The nightgown is the last of me, she was also my first.

TIME IS A BRIDE

Married to the woods. Once,
A man grabbed her by the Talk—
Her only knowing. Thereafter, she
Grew tall, the hills were nothing-
Loomings, the doom was in her.
She pet her *sāwol* on Sundays.

There is no wandering ache
In fairy tales. They have the look
Of history: sealed as fruit, born
And beared, away. And words
Can be so round, she thought,
Givable, and in a basket. Carried
To a crone, not for comfort

But for Being. She was a *lȳtel* story,
On a pony bright and white as she,
Alone, and uncaring of this, ultimately.
All day long she kneaded a Myth—
Fragrant, though she never tasted it.
All Myths are saltless, she moaned,
And listened for what happened next.

Sometimes she dressed up in Fame.
She lit up the woods in her flameless
Costume. No one saw. She liked her well
Of clear, cold water turning dark. Knots
Were interesting to her, and knives to cut
Them with. The mind, a knuckle to be
Gnawed. Flesh and bone, no secrets at all.

Her mynde was Work.
Her beings were her own.

THUMBELINA

after Yuliya Lanina's music box "Thumbelina"

Thumbelina is a racehorse, muddy, bloody,
Rolling in and out on the Toad's tongue,

A joy-diamond for the choking. Lanuginous
Bride. Planeterium howl

Wounding summer's bark. Walks into a room
And everyone surges out their feet,

Crabs or flowers scraping down the drain.
Approach, approach on your pretty paws

Says the mole, the beetle, and Thumb comes
Like an aneurism, a chandelier

Plugged into the wedding's socket, booming
Tulips. You're a wish, Thumb,

Even your mother stands at your rainbow's
End like a dark, abandoned hut . . .

Run, my Diamond, before the Toad swallows!
You're tiny to carry, tiny your cry,

An insect seizing her reason
For the first time—a sound

Of no consequence to giraffes,
Chewing the moon's soft yogurt with blind lips.

WEPT ALL DAY, DIDN'T KNOW WHY

Saints are those who do not live amongst the people.

When I first met a saint I placed it tenderly between
Two halves of a sandwich and left it to the wolves. Suchly
Did I observe that no animals came to eat it. At last
One deer pawed the sandwich and nibbled the bread.
Some birds came over to hold a slice up to the sky
Like a banner announcing God's glory. By this time

The saint was unclothed with its face in the dirt.

I felt sorry &

Shut it back into its walnut shell. I whispered sweet
Gospels. I made a proper burial for it on my tongue.
For a saint must die in its own language. Then

I was like, Okay, and drove home

In my imaginary vehicle splattered with bird droppings.
I became small from crying. A pulley system geared
Until it snowed inside of me. Good grief I said. It was time
To bring my hands together over a woman's body and worship.
Time to turn off all the faucets God had forgotten about.

Long is my journey to all the empty restaurants crammed into a walnut
     shell.

Irreversible is my decision to eat the browned defeated apple
On my way to the bathroom. Now nobody knows me. Not even God
Knows me, He who pares his fingernails my whole life long.

Like the saints I will now be stingy with my love &

Pave a road out of myself so it may be traveled by those
Hungry for bread. Night, reckon us back into the original loom.
Braid our hair into the branches so we cannot move,
So we may be happy.

If you see a saint in the road please put it back.

EUNUCH

He is a caveat in the glut of it. A thumbprint.
Omnivore with nothing to eat, he folds his hands.
He steps one foot, then another, into a pair
Of hairy vowels, gets stuck. It's the little
Stitches that hurt most, it's the buttons.
Language is blind, a worm threading in and out.
Unleashed unto him was a violent piety, a herd
Of suckling pigs splattering and swolling him.
Great Wrongs and Mercy did hold him down,
And he never got up from where he lay,
The wood darkened under him night and night.
Language moves by feeling; it finds unseeing
Holes. His wound not dim but distant, a lightbulb
Left in a closet, from which he coughs. He watches
A virgin exit the church. Her beauty is a single
Plump word squealing in between the pews,
Leaving behind a sticky streak, marmalade or dew.

LADY BUTTER

Her hand a country
Where women are fools
In harrowing bonnets,
Only dreams can pursue them.

Winter bullied her, forced
A finger in her, made her

His wife, so that nobody
Could touch her. When crowned,
She magnified her wand

Into a mirror, caught what wind
And wired it shut. Her nature
Ballooned in a cave of iniquity,

So beautiful
Windows closed at her arrival
And true became truest
Just by looking at her.

Her *her* a burr, the burr of her.

The waiting & bleeding
Trembled her over, the monster
Of her and her might—
Origin Unknown.

A man with no business wearing a hat
Got lost in the woods, and took her:

Her names were Luxury, Glory,
Little Worm. She carved a carriage
And suffocated in sated sleep.

What a dull, what a little dull, what
A dull little being she was.
It is not up to us, who lives in the window.
Her mongrel's puddled drool a portal

To nowhere. Afraid to move, afraid
Of her body with its bells and chambers, echoing.

THE HOBBLER

Call the Hobbler, that crude hive, spilked
Large in hoard and deed, heath hoared
And shoveled, hair bathed in gravel, mead.

Hobbler, will you bake in your mind
A speechcake? The beginning of life
Palpitates in you, milds. The Hobbler

Frightens children; she is hungry as grass.
But she bears treats for us, her maw-sighs
Make a stinging symphony. The Hobbler

Is a princess, too: her cats, the Minkles,
Commune with trash, and she watches
TV through their aluminum antennae.

How joyous it is to be the Hobbler!
She rides a moose into the garden and thinks,
And everything she watches thinks, too.

When night comes, she is cold and blue.
Every morning, she lives again. Her true
Wonder, though, is this: No one made her.

Neither in space nor sky nor soil was she born
To mother or father. She boiled from her own brain
Once—and spoke, and then spoke again.

THE PRIEST

He listened to an opera called, "The small
Hole through which I watch you." His hands
Smelled like medicine. Some dangerous thing
Approached, or maybe he was just hungry,
A spear in his belly. He was always the Least
In the room, he simpled his hair in the mirror,
Wishing and washing the wish in a dirty creek;
The wood of her, he wanted to unlock it,
For her watery mane like a pitcher poured
Mournings into him from swollen stars. His
Serious self wore a turtling light out on the town,
And he so honest he never took his shoes off, even
Before God,—but it was the Being he was after,
The Be spinning on empty fruit dishes when no
One was looking, though he got up earlier
Everyday to catch it, and he wanted the key
To turn in him too and bring the spill of pungent
Tarred language, lit. Years later he realized
He'd already buried it alive, the Language,
Without meaning to,—but it had followed him
around so, sweating into his collar and bringing all
The wrong women (no She), and when it was near
His mind wept and held conferences with armoires
—And when it was gone, he let the lightwood
Of himself go up in flames, adding his own
Pollution to the thick of the already-dinge,
Shooting down whatever bird was most plentiful.

HIGH PRIESTESS

God split me and fried a snake down my middle,
In plain view of me which gasped, in oil. He
Tore the serpent tongue, boiled and chewed it,

Littered the cup, drunk walking, the dew closed
Its eyes when God yelled. Meanwhile, the snake
Digested dragonflies and moths. He aged

Jealous as a river. Wanting coins, wanting sleep.
He jawed my kneecap and sucked my marrow
Until a grass patch grew up his brain and pierced

The skull. His eyes famished & ants ate of him.
At this point I was two days old. Itch of insects
Inside cleaning the corpse. For a year I drank

Sugar water with strenuous love. A pig carried
Me to the next clearing. A green taste in my mouth.
Tongue green, blood green. I saw everything

Is a sheep standing in pasture, sunwarm and rank.
Straw. The good grass people. Whirrings in wood.
In my cupboard, I took out the good pitcher.

OUR LADY OF THE ROPES

Her mind roped idle inside its sore bonnet,
Harnessed a sphere to catch fire the woods
And so famished a wreath around her, good

Clearing for dinner. She lassoed loss—its
Big spoony eyes and body large as pasture—
And crunched that cricket in between her teeth.

How she rode the haunted carapace then!
Her sunflower-eating brain unhooking its dress,
Crawling mad, unbuttoned, through history's

Rotten math. And hurting to see it so, her mind
Begged to be out, then feared to be homeless,
Didn't want that begging—Instead, she washed

The burnt land careful from a silk pail. Thinkers
Bloomed, generous as mud! Holding shoes up
To their ears to hear her message, which is thus:

I say to the ache
In ache's mouth,
I say to the ache
In armor, I say
Take the armor

Off, peek flat-out into mine own heart.

TAPESTRY WITH MAIDEN

My braids swim
With moat alligators
Who love such tinsel
Brushing their backs.
My beauty is mechanical,
A hairless clock or hairy
Cabinet. My mood purples
In a stable. None dare
Approach unless beastly,
Chaliced, jewel groined.
I am processioned by rats,
We walk into a country
Of men who eat live fish
And trees who sink
Into the soil at night.
Queen wants me look up
At her from the cloth.
Rather eat my own rag.
My mind is wet, I touch it.

HIEROPHANT

The Hierophant has six legs. Octopus legs,
Mare-riding-into-the-gloomy-sunset legs.
He visits in shawls, he is a woman. Come
Have a quail egg, he says, Come have a bear
In the shape of a duck. Duck transmogrified,
With antlers... All day long little umbrellas
Of doubt settle on him and populate his back.

On holidays he says, "I am shovel implanted
In the Lord's forehead." Then sings, polar bear
Taking a bath, ant wandering his own spine.
The similes are smiles crawling his dead body,
He picks them off. Surrounded by the evil
Language, he loses one leg hair at a time.

KROSHECHKA HAVROSHECHKA

after Yuliya Lanina's music box "Kroshechka Havroshechka"

I wish you a snout, a dead fish coat
So stinky no one will touch you.
Teach you to fry evil eyes in a pan.
Grant you a taste for plunderage,
Milk down the chin. But even the fish
Coat weeps, looking at you: A child
Smuggled from plural winter, a girl
Tossed out from thrashing nurseries.
Hostile geometry. Georgic sorrows.
Tail scraped, nailed to the barn.
So I became a medicine storm. Gave
You a hiding place between my ears.
Stepped into my own murder basin
So Prince might eat my bone fruit.
Still you fall through the Great Yawn.
Cow is a hide pinned open to passing
Winds, the unshut eye of the cosmos.
My language marks your forehead—
The hoofprint blinks with perceptive
Rain. Even now, I am working on you.

HERMIT

Hermit is twig house and black tiger
Blood, circulating. Daily he unhooks
Sun from sun as a crow does. Soups
Tickbites for supper. Bleeds all night
For the revolving suns, for the sound
Of lichen growing on another continent.
Hermit heats his kettle of salamanders.
He was born in this robe of dust, milk,
Where fish swim and peek out his collar.
A wandered sheep said to him: Spooky.
Hot strange Monkey plays piccolo
In his forest. And Brother Snow-Crab
Climbs a mountain, weeping, no one
Has ever seen him…Hermit is twigs,
Tiger bread, and a little knife of love.

THEN ALWAYS THE SEA

Always anger, like a shovel, left in the yard overnight;
Always someone's cat, dead under a heap;
Always a gnome crossing the castle lawn, counting his whiskers;
His money made from old shoes, stolen and gilded;
Always a rooster in the wagon, hiding, keen to capture;
Always a lady, wary of capture, pinned to the grass;
The sea full of rings, the sea full of itself and other people's hair,
And the worms in the earth watching us, the sound turned off;
The sea trapped in its own body, randy, despised in a new wig;
Hallelujah, say the children, who have grown and are waking,
Their toes and skin in place, and nothing missing;
Something sloshing through them, briny, not of themselves;
The sea carrying diseases, mangy as a dog, rising, never crashing;
The children under one fur, black and lustrous as lawn,
The gnome petting;
If the sea can't stop
Looking in the children's mirror, riding their ponies,
Slapping their limits, washing their caves, making marrow
Of their femurs, handprints where their hands should be,
Filling their towers;
Then always the sea, and the panther's fur;
Always the myth, placenta in the panther's mouth;
Buried, tamped down in the yard;
The children go still as a party, and back to sleep;
The painting goes on, shifting her roots, her branches.

RABBITCATCHER OF MY MOODS

There is no such one and no hat from which
The rabbits come. And who are the rabbits
Anyway who leap so elegantly through all
My hoops and lassoes. Once, abundance.
Then, hollow. What robes do I wear. Does nothing
Remain. How do I be brave in the face of it.
Stand here with my hands lifted and take it.
I know it will come. I know my heart is the shape
Of the devil's tongue. That he wants to plunge
His tongue into my chest I know. And here come
The locomotives: toy train of shame, train of lust,
And the train that runs me down every time.
I have to be planted in the springbeds to wake up.
But I must do a gratitude dance for jam and butter,
Toast and peaches, love and hats, rats and makeup,
Licks, pits, tits, bright buses, showers, arrogance.
O fulsome gulp I bow down to you. You rabbished
Me in the hidden woods and I became the genius
Of the cabbage patch. You pull on my sleeve:
Sometimes nothing in there, sometimes bloodsigh,
Sea gardens. My stunning begged bedraggled moon
Followed me out of bed where I've been spooned
And sucked into a song for days. Become a dazzle,
Hot burner on the stove. Spring cracked me open
Like a sprout. No time for undelight. I need
Reigns but who will hold them? Rabbits don't
Have hands and neither do I. Out of my sleeves
Came nothing again. I have one basket only
And lay eggs just once a year. The rest I sleep.

MANY LIVES

Married to the butcher I grew happy on meats,
Marinating in juice when meeting neighbors.
They thought I smelled good, licked the salt
Off my arms. Next was poaching a robin's egg
To marry the chick inside once its blue-green
Eye-rings subsided. Jealous rage, jealous rage
Of the sea filled my mouth with bitter. Then
There was a hold on me of indisputable calm.
I married the baker's daughter after a fortnight
Of chasing her slow through Elysian fields
On quiet fire. Maidens carried water beacons
To me, I was loved in my belief that angels
Are dead yetis revived. I bled all over the place
And was deemed virgin. Finally, I wed a boar
Who trampled my hands until they became
Transparent, useless for anything besides
Magnification of butterflies and other such
Nonsense, grave nonsense. All my many lives
Grew into my feet like bamboo, and I worried
They wouldn't like me once they reached
My heart, which had sailed away on a ship
Of bombast, of frankincense and myrrh.
Preached unto myself and consecrated, I
Wore veils and pig snouts round my wrists,
Christened and astonished by various wiles,
Helped and stewed, long beautiful hair flowing
Out of the tips of my hair, for I was perfect,
For blank and moving people came from far
And wide to touch my face for luck and grief.

CAN I BE A MAN OF GOD?

I've been drinking from the wrong cup.
Cup of gold for a king to sip
Till his insides gild and soul pebbles.

Deep green, potion
Me over.

Deprivation, too, soaks the soil:
Strange bulbs waddle up.

My praise boat dissolves in the river.

My staircases lose squires.

No one will suffer
Absent my creeping.

The milk marshes,
My eyes jewel,
Breakfast calls me to the window

Where birds take residence

In my chest
And the little wormings, I do love.

NOTHING SCARES ME

Like my parents' death, so I made this horse
Out of spit and childhood scribblings
And he warbles in his branches.

Washing dishes,
He wears an apron with a window
To the lawn

Where phosphorescents leap.
The horse is
Sad, is mine.

The future opens me, a cabinet
For a horse to put his head inside
And lick.

Mama, Papa, I would whittle
My ribs into rollercoasters for you
To ride down the death hole,

If you would like
You could live inside the horse's skull—
Are you trying to kill me? —My mother's

Laughter tumbles with death's
Good clothes in the dryer
Down the hall from where I sleep.

A SMALL MAN GATHERS TWIGS IN THE BLACK HOUR

Mothers came out to hang up linens for the bats
To wear as wedding dresses. We were watching
TV and eating plaster, thinking about the storms
Our ancestors wore into battle to protect their wives
And bars of soap. For dinner we boiled a mad
Man's shoes in milk; the questions wound around
His ankles made strings in the soup. We turned
Off all the lights, as the hail was coming and our
Carapaces were ready for take off into space
Where we would surely be met by pleasant tribes
Offering us our own heads. I loosed my tongue
Into the streets where it wanders to this day
In its many coats, unused to being cold and alone.
Sitting on a park bench, then gathering twigs.

READER

I am a swineherd; I herd a black ocean
Today. The Only ships in me, and I am sunk.

Hooded reader, your puzzlement is
A brilliant net with which to catch many fishes.
May your head be one of the caught and carried

Home. Have you traveled in a winecasket
This long night? I arrive, Century-dead,
In the hallway where the Language hangs

On hooks. Reader, do not torture the wind.
Captive, it shifts in a barrel out at sea.
Slowly dying, it turns its dark, cogent mind.

TWELVE DAYS OF WEDDING

How you grow my hairs from your own body.
How you pull them out until I am nothing.
How my love transpires into wind.

At the deep of me is a graveyard of live
Cabbages. The cabbages are so good,
Especially in the sea hour. Their scales

Slink dangerous as your feral cat garden.
Our wedding gifts have long, worn monkey
Arms, they swat from the branches.

The antelopes in my eyes feed and feed
On your beauty. Your beauty is catching,
All my antelopes are on fire and ruined.

The future wears furs,
Carries an icicle.
Open her robe,

And you'll see her body is a dull knife,
Her heart a bell jar beating with a clock.
She bites us open, my cabbages moan

And swim back to the sea. I have no dead
Yet, my net teems with splendid fish.
It is heavy to have so much, heavy
To eat so many feasts before they spoil.

EVERYONE IS WELCOME AT A WEDDING

Nerves shark up my loved ones' pistils.
Would that they were barnacle-armoured.
I live in a creamy ramekin, I touch no one,
My ramekin is a UFO, it charms, calls out
The slithery wolves: Bring me my goblets.

Death is making my friends sassy
Enraged flowers, red spiky sewer-mad,
Seasick and rocking the feast table.
Loss was an old man who looked like a father,
And it was cold out, so they let him in.

I too will age: small wounds on my body
Will open into larger wounds, I will take
Showers for all the wrong reasons.
And yet I will have made a little lake,
Each year-juice spilling in: Look!
Even now a sturgeon leaps from it.

My love and I marry in two days. Death
Can't touch us now. Can only tip his glass
To us at the bar as we wine in our finery—
O it was all worth it for eating creams
In our finery!—and we toast him back,
As he looks a little like my father, and how
I miss my father, wish he were here.

BLOOD HARE

Now that I am married, I go
To the water and suffer

At its feet. The water is a beaked thing,
Very serious.

What of the little world covered in wounds?
What of the summer I slept on?
The winter is vast

And behind us. It misses us
And waves.

Blood hare
Is what it means to have one's dearest
People far away, and many imposters near.
One peers deeply into irrelevant cuts
And boils on one's hands.

My youth is a severed hand! It bleeds
Gloriously, then shovels its own grave!
I've given up the mood

And the window is dull as porridge.
You see,

I have made a career of mishearings
And sink my most precious statues
In the bog.

BECAUSE I AM A THICK BROAD

How now will the King, forthwith grown legion?
Where will I my pastries, with which fat to become?

I took the garbage out, and ate it well
With raccoons envying by and by.

The pain everywhere evaporateth and becometh
None: How could anything ever go wrong,
Now that I am married, and have birthed my third

Toad? Sweet are my toad suppers into the moonlight.
Tough are the stalks of the Matriarch
In childhood grass now growing again.
Fever in the loins of horses doth fuel my lust

This summerwide. Where do you think I now,
Back damp with mud dimming the morning Stars?

(No one beckoned once—horrors ensued—I loved whores
Of nonsense and painterly Europe—the piecemeal troubled—
The Lord, miffed with me, did soften his eyes for a season,
Such making immutable wrongs rope with blood my body—)

But all is over now.

So Why in the reckoning did you bring me hither
To this here cookout, and did your head come off
Seeing bees in someone's backyard of feelings?

A silent space to sit with you and be hungry now
After blubbering my way through pith and toil
In a sieve of meat, my love, Immortal

And I tell the truth.

HUSBAND, I AM A SCARY CAULDRON

All I ever wanted was to be a thing on fire
You could put out in the sink. I put my face
Inside the word *poor* and lay there till crustacean.

Now I am happy to be your cactus. I have little
Cactus dreams, and troubling nightmares I telegraph
To Pope through a passageway in my flowerpot;
We luncheon there, in the tunnel betwixt—
"How was your supper yesteryear?" "Doingly,
And yours?" "Too much blood I suppose, well."

I lick the walls of my limitations; I love them
As I love you. You and I both taste like plaster,
The mice inside the plaster, and the ghosts inside
The mice. Lucky to be dead, lucky to have lived.
I commissioned Mayor Goblin to hammer us

Into a locket. Now all we need is a root vegetable
Fairy to take us to the marriage station. My mother
Places her soul over our eyes and says, Be well,
Be well. My heart decomposes at the rate of a whale's.

Husband, you are the doll's house I crawl into
And the grass loud on fire outside. The dog laps
At the fire; it is his belly sufficed. I am taller than
I've ever been but I can hear everyone's cancer
Growing. We wake nightly and are barely bodied,
Or slim bodied, or silver bodied, or are branches
In the silver streets. In the morning I will feel better.

THE WILD FREEDOM OF BEING UNLOVED

By day, I am a PraiseBeast and my mouth is wet.
I eat all the cakes: they were made for me:
Everything was: there is no other way.

Down in my Thinkies,
I think.
Tending

The little seeds, I grow a peasant
Bottom amongst expensive onions

And meat. My dog is sad eternal, therefore
I sleep. And before sleep,

I have the kind of dream
I can hide under a pot
When the husband gets home.

I feel widow-like,
The *Is* is bitter today.

It is unfair to be so glamorous. *"She fainted*
And passed away under the burden of much envy,"
Wrote all the reputable sources,

But Ah! they wrote in vain. They should have said,
"She sweated much.

And once found a spacehole connecting us to God.
Whispering there nightly,
Tell me about the crests and rivers,

Tell me I am a medieval queen,
Tell me about the ankle tongs and the clad,
Tell me true and brave,
All the while kneeling down."

SATURDAY EVENING

It's itching out, my feet are raining.
My Magellan sank into the soil long ago, cracked the earth's egg.
I am a ferocious brood, my milk has fed an army.
Only my arrogance can save me, it gleams in the dark.
Waking nightly I am too large for my house.
There are giants in the dry creek, swinging
Their arms as they stroll, muscles taut with purpose.
They have already won the earth, and no one knows.
I want to tell everyone,
Wake you up,
Your torso splitting with kitchen light,
Your glasses crooked, lens fractured,
Hot milk burning your throat.
I love you, it is very clear.
I'll follow you, we'll keep chasing each other.
The call in the dark and the call.
Labyrinths rising and thickening,
We can demolish them later.
And always peace in the ancient tile
House. My husband, you gold
Round locket with no hinge,
No inside, just the whole.

SHOULD WE HAVE A BABY?

I've made a hawk of my every cell:
Beaks pointed at you, they rush forward.
Husbands and wives is a long road to dinner
On winter.
How dark the dark is in the dark.
They lean their heads into the windshield,
Half full of sleep.
I've only ever been two eyes and a jaw,
The rest of me a cloak.
A robe always open
Like a brain blown out.
They are straining towards what is coming,
What is coming is snow.
A tongue should curl them,
Live them in Most Forgotten Alaska.
How small they look.
I have no control over anything.
Somebody dropped a watch in the tundra,
My blood beats in its face.
At the house, you put your hands up my cloak
Where my body should be.
The absence thrills,
Like stepping into ice where a river
And then fire is.

I VISIT MY ORACLE

By me, I mean the Thousand-Eiyed Beast,
Lacquered, tumoured, and nailed—shapely.
By woods, I mean Arachnoids, lecherous,
Starved, transparent. By her, I mean big
As a moon, Miss Moorage, eyes resting
In the usual milk, dusty-Brain'd so that I
Must wipe it, so that she may aspire
For me a word into the glass goblet—
Stir it, gelatinous, into a Meaning.

Tenders, governs, she does, says I am
Too hasty to make a herd of Languages.
Decease! She says into a pot, and they
Drop and mewl. *How conscious*, she says,
Muttering, *Too conscious*—it's all too much
For her. She slides back into her slipper,
Crunches insects eyelessly in a tavern.

I go home galoshed, stank all up my being,
Far from oracled, my haruspex a minx,
When at woods' edge I trip over a loosed
Burl of a word (how did she trap me so,
Cobwebbed as she is?)—and moment, feel
Me step through myself—but that's a lie,
And the trees snicker like they never knew me.

SPEAK PLAINLY! (A DEMAND)

I speak plain: good
Night. Supper is on.
Aurora masterpieces
My hair: lifts it once
Like a little summer, cup
My smell, nose in it.
Ear, I've discovered, is
A storm to enter, no
Return. Ordinary meals
Made me who I am
Plus occasional fish
Skull spilling eye. I
Speak plain: as bald
Wind in a bald house
Quieting bald children.
Every journey is an
Egg to fall asleep in
So the earth quakes.
Beg of me a word so
Vibracious, I can't—

SHE SPITS & TOUCHES HER TONGUE TO HER LUNGS

I was outside myself, picking corn in a tall shadow,
When I was ordained to be an Anglo-Saxon
Warrior making my head from my own head, making
An extraordinary instrument from which we shall
All suffer madly. And the mirror was always a jewel,
And the jewel is a spun armor of living tigers, who
Clamber out and slurp your oyster heart, a task
To be shouldered by barbarous cardinals,
And in thick-smirched, burning loams of carpentry
I was castled to be a moat woman in my own
Brain: when mice come in, she runs out: the worlds
Are large, the openings small and this big fish
In herself is what she is, this vision, this fishling
Gold, the seventh and the big fool and she does
Eat the meat and she does not uncreature
Herself at any point of the calendar, she is a tall
Seamstress thinking doomingly, she a brave loss,
And did you brilliant the flies making swimming
Dialect at your feet, did you subtract from your eyes
Heavy spoons placed upon the mood-mood,
Did you crouch down holy in the you of you,
Did you crouch, did the crouching make a crackle
And did long-suffering beads crowd themselves
Into your dark dream sockets? I am under duress
Of flames but believe you me that certain flowers
Toss their rings into nighttime and so become
Crowned by ancient unseen kings in the halo
Where my genius did roam and wear little
Inkles, and the animals have eaten my numbers.

ANGLO-SAXON

Dear moss murk.
Dead dazzle moon.
Better than any orphrey,
Osier, or oubliette.
Thrall town:
Day curse:
I wive you.
Dark other in my deep,
Every whip of you
Is a good bleed.
Your mood-spear
Eyes me, reads me.
Each ask, ash,
Gathers me under
As a sooth ache.
Sieve me your ear.
Feed me your eat.
Tread on my sorrow
Until it stones, blinds,
Clothed in your oath.
Your death root
Pins me gut to earth.
You are the think
Thorning me. Your
Weight my deed.
Nothing weeps me
Like your spring.

SOLACER

Each English word hoards spitted
Fishbones from a dungeon supper.
Language wrenches, tongues me,
Scyllas my backspine for a wig,
Vertebra crown, goons my scalp—

The rest is musk
The rest is muster

Quick it was, such a luck serpent-struck my artery, and boiling
Before the serving, I crawled
From my Open Neck, and announced to all the guests—

&

How the moon storied after.
So that I stood, alchemied.
My carriage forked, molten.

I, a Sloe-eyed maiden in comely
Woods: harvesting blakkened roam.

Spoken castle, I am always washing.
Little as bristle—but thinking, thinking.

Snow heaps on my captured
Shoulders, I have walked the circumference
Of myself. Plant grasses; wait.

ANGLO-SAXON (2)

Clever is not an Anglo-Saxon word.
Neither *coward* nor *nurture* nor *enemy*.
Weep was theirs, *sleep* and *wean*—always
The weaning off sweet milk to wake.
But they felt as much as they worked:
Soul was theirs, carved and hammered
From stones. We are left with the stubs
Of their speech: it molds in our gardens.
No *solar*, but *sun*: no *space*, only *bog* and *spread*.
They knew *knew* first and best. Knew
To spill and spare. They found *play*
In *plegian*: the *g* ground up with earth,
Vowels splashed with dark wine. I
Am a bride to the speak they bedded,
Rotted, and grew: made new for me in *slough*,
Dog, and *watching*. They gave me the *What*,
First word of the oldest tale, the *What* I hoard
And cannot keep, the *What* I carry now to you.

WHAT DO ASPARAGUS DREAM OF?
THEY DREAM OF BLOOD

From this hollow plain I make a thicket, I make
The wind engrave my eyes. I wear a bearsuit,
Cunning banquet, a century pummeled by speed,
Panhelic. Shaman says, Stop looking at that bag
Of bleating potatoes you call a self, that house
Swimming from its windows. I wander at night,
A tiger with no hooves. A nerve of meat chewed
To death by horses. I tried to destroy myself,
Whirling, prodding refrigerators and offspring,
Drinking jars of buttons. Then Toad surfaced
From the grass to say: I don't know much. Well
Neither does this arm, which follows me around
With impudence, with the grace of circus newts.
Leaping turnips, stationary gods, godlookalikes:
I need to make something of this puny, hogstruck,
Unwanted day. Your beauty's apparel shimmies
Across the floor. You covered up your nakedness
With poetry and a pear. Venerable mares,
I am the Several. Plum and gorge. I suppose
Your hours are haunting and delicate as trees,
As jewelry. And your rapt attention afraid of itself
Like women rotating azaleas. This rabbit's ears
Tell me you have many secrets of your own.
My pigfeet progress towards the Golden Opening,
And I spit out the pairings of goose and goose
As some kind of elegant beetle colonizes my audio.
Asymmetrical Muses in Syrupy Dresses, it is I,
The Lemon Tree, having raked tawdry lumps
From my eyelashes for years, hoping you'll notice.
My Bees, sleepy in Victorian frocks, share sacred

Rages within teacups. And you, Unintended Bulb
Of Reason, why do you erect in my Napoleonic roots?
Eye-sized seeds in a land where no one grows.
The stud in the mind. For a donkey to lick. Hangs
Stalled and stony. Better than a pinprick. Keep
Away from mirrors, says Shaman—O Shaman,
Only you have loved my buried, crepuscular face.

GOODNIGHT, SOLILOQUY

Oven off.
TV stilled.
Spine blind.
Roots told.
Fly drowned.
Fields molten.

Tired of feeling everything, the lake takes no more prisoners.

May ancient wars travel your brow, may the skulls of jaguars call you
    with their emperors,
Green nerves, liquid tesseracts, goodness spooling—

May you wake
Bellied, deserted.
Years gathered.
Feet mended.
Being steeled.
Guardian howled.

Emerge from the milky eye.
Held as you are by no one in particular, loose in the hands.

THE MIRACLE SMACKED ME

Did you just speak to me as if to a horse?
As in, trying to sow seeds with your hair
In my knickers? I've embellished my knickers
With thinking, now they wink knowingly
At whomsoever passes. The snow in their eyes
Gleams, too, a snow that waits for the moose
To arrive. (The moose are larger than your mind.)
Gertrude Stein cradles me in her arms. "You
Are the ugliest baby I've ever seen," she coos,
Sounding just like a rhinoceros clearing its throat
In the last moment of extinction. *Well.* Those trees
Are contagious! I live and sway inside them.
My mind is a golden marsupial, forever
Nibbling on something in the musty pouch.
The stars worry, they are sorry. But I am not.
I am a live nerve, caught by something huge
And serious, but watch—still I keep on flying.

NO IFS OR BUTS, ONLY ANDS

I want aggressive steeples and dilated apples.
Travel me there, golden burro in a blurry hat.
A narthex of litigious bugs follows me instead.
Someone cradles my head from far off with long,
Long arms. I've devoted my life to pisciculture,
Finally. Piston of me goes bludgeoning. But I like
Everything! This and that door says, Life Is Hard,
But my steps through the garden are gigantic!
Sunflowers are ripe with the seed of ancestral lions!
My seven uneducated dragons are bitter regarding
Their fortunes, and can you blame them! My hair
Is loops of live tigers resuscitating! Each pinprick
Reveals a new eye in my splendid skin, marvelous
Pie bringing out the Fungoid. Failure like nervous
Houses lathers me over. Trees of disappointment—
Urgent, pharmaceutical, farming the patriarchy
—Mop up the lather. It's true, this lollipop future,
Just as my unshackled head galumphs eloquent
As wine, working for its keep in the haystacks
(Haystacks, I see you, you spiritual virgins).
Latinate logic stews in my plum. Lines crisscross
The world, a child running with bright yarn.
Thunder is my keeper. I'm in the porchlight
With the muskrat, who steps into the circle of time
With no clothes on, no candle to touch the sea.

SONG OF MY SELF-LOATHING (PART ONE)

I could suck the sweat from my socks and live off the salt for a
thousand years.

I could make houses from my snot, and if soldiers were to come and
stomp all over my toes they would die before completing their task,
such is the hideous number of my appendages.

If all the marbles of my shyness were released into the streets, no one
would ever walk upright again.

If everyone else's eyeballs went dim, the sum of that low-wattage
couldn't hold a dead lightbulb to the darkness of my vision.

Whole villages have been killed picnicking in the minefields of my
atrocities.

I am so self-loathing that I cannot continue, but I will continue out of
self-loathing.

Under the law and muck of my confusion I go running.

I place cold hands on my back, and remove them, and call myself home
to the tiny dark oven of myself,

Where my self-loathing is king and queen and walks with a nightstick
in its hands.

Drunks give fumbled toasts to my foolishness,

And toasters are dumped daily into that river, already thick with dead
dogs and lined with raccoons washing their hands.

As I have only located three thoughts in my entire skull, I conclude that instead of brains I have an enormous whale spilling out of my head, slapping at the shore.

Children are afraid of the lopsided way I walk, trying to hold the whale in.

Only the most awkward of birds attend to me, the pelican, the dodo, the heron.

Once my self-loathing was wrapped in newspaper and carried in the arms of an old woman across the street.

But my self-loathing quickly swallowed the newspaper, the old woman, and the street. It is swallowing all of us right now.

There are ballrooms of empty coatracks for every time I did not come to the aid of another.

Forests where books run rampant, raised by wolves because I never opened their pages.

No one escapes the hounds running from the hills of my self-loathing.

My self-loathing is large enough to be a shelter to all, a tent city of refugees.

For I planted my self-loathing in the right season, and it grew immense and gorgeous.

THE MINISTRY OF CROWS

This is the black field my shame drains to,
Where a lady burnishes her face, hiding
In a shawl. Every time a mean thing is said,

The field widens and someone falls in.
The Ministry of Crows circles over, scavenges.
I walk the perimeter and win a cake. Clap clap

Black applause and I go bobbing for apples
In a black river. I lay the paint on thick
So it can live on my wall forever. My ear

Against the world is. My ear against the world
Is dull. But brightening. Wincing traveller,
To wear red shoes in this life is to eat cinnamon

In the next. To die by bear now means a heavy,
Well-haired heart later. Today is moms and TV,
Tomorrow is milk and walks along a dragon's back.

Wisdom, you popped out like a prairie dog,
Then left a husk. Are you mammal
Or snake? Friends with everyone or no one?

My ear is pressed against foul winds. My eye
Wanders to the twigs. The Ministry of Crows says:
Swollen with river will be your thirsty bushels.

MY EVIL POTATO

Wouldn't it be lovely to make a million dollars and feed
No one but myself, for hours, in a high lonely castle
Of brocade and crimson, my head a fishhead drooling,
Antlers growing out of my legs, my tongue
Parchment unrolling over the soup?

In the black wood outside, the roaming
Becomes a girl gathering red currants.

My evil potato sprouts eyes
And limbs. We go walking arm in arm
Through the forest and into the desert,

Where a figure brings hungry water to a dry cloak,
Where the dark hungers after the desert water,
Where the water is cloaked in dry hunger.

ORIGIN STORY

I was born into a shopping cart, pushed through a parking lot
By a manic aunt. I was just a skeleton then, but already waving
Like a mayor, though only the secret trashcan women were out.
My aunt's eyes were wild, she had insane wheat brewing
The field over, she'd spent all her money on overpriced
Notebooks, her torso was woozy with bad decision Tetris.
I cowered, my skeleton pelvis rattled against the metal cart.
Oddly, the trees weren't changing much, no matter how far
We ran, they all sang the same nursery rhymes and patted
Me down with their big hands. I had my first rash of beauty
When the night began slow dancing with a whistle from
Earlier in the evening, which remembered itself as we passed.
The whistle laughed in the night's arms. With a pang I knew
This romance would end, whistle and night would become
Simple farmers, combing our foreheads over with rakes,
But the pang eased as I thought of human extinction and
The slow growth of species over the earth, its face restful
As a mother turning on the microwave. So gradually, over
The course of the shopping cart ride, I learned to speak
In a manner hospitable to plants, in a manner hospitable
To humans and the cows who raise them from the dead,
In a manner that wouldn't embarrass my windmill and cause
Him to cover his eyes with his arms. The convenience store
Milk jugs were sweating, and the parking lot dog's head
Was an angry basket of flowers, considering. I could feel
My aunt getting tired at last, we'd been running forever,
And by the time my childhood ended, my aunt, she was gone.
How the worms moaned and turned over in their living
Graves that night! I walked home in electronic rags,
As if Zeus had ripped up a lightning bolt to make me,
A loose collection. The flower-dog was now a toilet

Calm and white; then a refrigerator, murderous with
Weight, groaning with meaning; then a bunch of forks
Dumped into the sink at once. The vibe was decidedly
Domestic but I was still learning the ways of the world,
So I tied ribbons over my face, fell asleep in my own palm.
When I woke up, whatever is out there, always ranging,
Sniffed me over at great length, like I was an angel
Carved from soap, or a trash woman bearing secrets
From her nighttime vigil, and that feeling of being sniffed
Over, head to toe, that's what I've been after ever since.

POVERTY BUCKET

Have I sold my soul to that devil No-Money?
Would I be better off with a cow for a job?
These are the questions, my friends. Shakespeare
Trades my wintry impulses for his own bulge.
It all comes from somewhere, especially the legs.
I'm wearing my tuskalicious bangles today.
I'm wearing that wooden heart I knocked out
Of an oak to the lunch party. I have festooned
Myself with galleries. Once I had plenty of cape,
But even so the wind from my apocalypse
Bicycle blew the velvet open, I never felt safe.
Today, like a carcass in heels, I have found
My Purpose—to rot in a valley of conservative
Gnats. I do, after all, have one kid in the pouch
And fourteen dogs vacillating round my wrist,
Ceiling fans in an Argentinian melancholy.
My friends! Why don't you come over anymore?
You do incomprehensible things in your kitchens
Without me. I thought we were in this together.
You tremble, cobwebs in the giant's dewy feet.
(I am the giant, and the feet.) The bitten apple's
Welling juice is my blood trying to reach you.
And that beautiful couple ducking under the trees
Of your swollen yard? My friends, that's me.

BOG PEOPLE

I miss how our poems would huddle together
At the imaginary buffet, not eating, bowing
Their heads in, wool coats making a village.
Today I hand out glitter crowns to beggars,
Tomorrow we're bog-bound, throats cut,
Noose-tied, snacks for the spring goddess.
That's all right—spring was always biggest.
Not the current-you but the forever-ago potato
I miss. Now you're a friend, but once you were
The Past, tinseled, storied, nosing with desire,
Happy shit thawing in the park. Our poems are
Dog's mercury, bracken, cinquefoil, goosefoot
Next to we, the faceless Danes. No personality,
I want to be the fungi crackling between trees,
The secret death-coin in a Viking's ear. Duck,
Handsome with blood, enough for everyone.
Let's meet for breakfast and shout: WE ARE
THE MEAT. No fear, just springtime, and
Our bones marking the outlines of the village.

ADMINISTRATIVE ASSISTANT

Have you observed how a shadow is simply
A giant's hair, swooping to and fro through time?
Sure, you could have a picnic there. There's a hulse
In the garden, back bare to the weeds and grackles.
I feel agitated, a cornucopia of stars with a snake
Inside. The snake's been having recurring dreams
Where it turns into a black branch and must grow
Very, very slowly. Like my beard growing long
And swaddling me, the dumpling, deep within.
Day after day I expect things to stay the same,
Have I learned nothing? I reject this land of small
Buckets never filled. My hummingbird companion
Lives here somewhere, which is a kind of comfort.
I must remember that money is not watching me,
Blind in its shifting burrow and never to be seen.
But my consciousness is looking, it has bundled
Itself into a filth pocket. What the drowned, honest
Rat says, I say, too. The black towel hides my horrible
Face. It is much irritable, how we are speaking now.
Last time we went to the well, my soul jumped
In, I watched. Then I pulled up the pail and drank.
My neck ajar, I poured my soul back in.

NIGHTWALK

Whatever else I seem to be doing, I'm actually

       always walking. At night. Without a head on.

    Isn't that crazy? Walking headless. And picking up apples.

                   The apples

are apples, but they're also things. Some are memories

    that won't come close, like deer, as one of us
          would be annihilated.

     One is the infinite absence of infinite friendship.

      Another is how what if I never wash my dishes well enough
and the spoons gather greasy residue for years and the kitchen bugs
    know about it and lick the spoons at night, and how
       even if the bugs won't lick them, the spoons
        will stay greasy forever and I'll go on living
         without ever fully appreciating this fact
           and then I die.

  Even that is an apple.

The relief of realizing this for the first time was so tremendous

    my hands almost fell off

       but I didn't let them, because then I would be
     handless as well as headless, and because

my hands wanted the chance to hold these apples,
                              they were greedy

                    for the size and weight of them.

            Antlers, time, little wantings.

I could put the apples in my basket.

            Antlers, time, and seaweed.

I could lick the apples, I could eat them.

            Soup, thought, bearing.

All the mead I ever wanted.

            Blood, and a making on a string.

The wildest most far-flung thing.

            Penchant, pension, peering.

I could leave them by a tree.

            Sequins, soldiers, sapphire.

I could leave them at the gate.

            Lamps, lamps calling black.

I could put them on my shoulder.

Meander, salamander, jokes.

I could cook them in a smolder.

Knowledge, pitchers, speech.

I could place them singing, each to each.

Lilies, mandarins, soot.

I could roll them over and around my foot.

Blame, shapes, magic.

They kept happening, and happened.

Bears, nudes, soap.

I could send them off to float.

Baskets, crusades, desire—

I gathered them sweetly around a fire.

And, Viking-wonderful, I helmeted on.

CRYPTOZOOLOGY

Geniuses crowd under the lake. Giants exist.
Giants exist at the mouth of the river. Inside trees
Are many desires but cutting the trees down
Won't loose them. Knowing things lie silent in mollusk
Shells. Mollusks don't know how to party. Bearded
Animals make no noise in the jungle. Middle-class
Warriors were carved from Stonehenge. Wigs
Are animals purring all over your head. Puddles
Everywhere if drunk from can turn you into pears,
Ghosts, or priests depending on the puddle.
Wonders, much like water, usually seek low places.
Cows have four stomachs and four ways
Of communicating with the gods. People have
Four eyes, two of which routinely roll away
To pleasant meadows so they don't have to see
Anything. The colorblind don't believe in God.
Spinal cords were made so demons might have
Something to hold onto. Slavs clutch their knee-
Caps more often than other types, rocking back
And forth. Smugness is a hockey puck waiting
To be kicked. Dragons once ate people inside
Of large earthy halos which is why volcanoes
Are so fussy and handsome. Whenever a fact
Is feeling frisky, it dunks its head in ice water,
Then eats a sweet potato. Some people are
Tragically unsilly because they have things
To lose. Chupacabras are mortally kind
To one another and certain species of turtle.
Millionaires are actually turtles with physics
Hats going on loopy. Some people have red faces
From too much cooking and moneymaking.

Even if one is a total failure, at least she will
Triumph completely in death. Cornfields have
Long haunted the hair roots of farmers. Jackets
Are for sex appeal plus feeling lonely in
While eating eggs. Sometimes squirrels cave
In and award kings with love eternal. Gold teeth
Are secret offerings to the gods. Kangaroos
Have a special gland that gives them imaginary
Orgasms. I am an imaginary orgasm is one way to put it.

READER (2)

You're eating yogurt; I'm an insect
At your feet. You wipe your hands
And peer. Part of you feels nothing,

A lively part of you wants to crush
My tiny intricacy. But I've got wings
And dart—catch me in your net,

And I'll admire your nose through the jar
In your bedroom. We'll share
The same nightmare in our sleep,

And if I hear you calling somewhere
I'll come running—I'll forget all
The ugly things we said, and we can wear

This plague of hornets like a cape,
March into town for a ham sandwich,
And be the shouting in the trees.

ACKNOWLEDGMENTS

Thank you to the following journals for publishing many of the poems in this book, sometimes in different versions.

Quarterly West, "The Folklore"
Black Warrior Review, "The Nightgown"
Gulf Coast, "Rabbitcatcher of My Moods"
CutBank, "My Evil Twin"
Tupelo Quarterly, "Kroshechka Havroshechka"
West Branch, "The Priest," "Eunuch"
Beloit Poetry Journal, "Poverty Bucket"
Fence, "Solacer"
The Journal, "Tapestry with Maiden"
The Adroit Journal, "Lady Butter"
Cimarron Review, "Our Lady of the Ropes," "The Hobbler"
Witness, "Time Is a Bride"
Guernica, "Twelve Days of Wedding"
Phantom Limb, "Wept All Day, Didn't Know Why"
The Missouri Review, "Saturday Evening"
jubilat, "Should We Have a Baby?"
Juked, "The Hurt Opera"
smoking glue gun, "Cryptozoology"
Pleiades, "Hour of Monks"
A Riot of Perfume, "Husband, I Am a Scary Cauldron"
Talking River, "Speak Plainly!," "Can I Be a Man of God?"
The Fairy Tale Review, "My Time with the Angels," "Administrative Assistant"
The Brooklyn Review, "Origin Story," "She Spits & Touches Her Tongue to Her Lungs," "The Ministry of Crows"

Thank you to the Interlochen Arts Academy for making me a poet, and to the James A. Michener Center for Writers for sealing the deal. To

Will Evans, Sara Balabanlilar, and Deep Vellum Publishing for taking me on, and to the Tasajillo Residency for letting me finish this book among feral hogs. Thank you to Michael Delp, for reading my first poems and dedicating himself so generously to my growth, and to all of my poetry teachers, who made such a difference: Michael Adams, Derick Burleson, Jack Driscoll, Dobby Gibson, Brigit Pegeen Kelly, Anne-Marie Oomen, and Dean Young. To former Michener director Jim Magnuson, for being such a pal. Thank you to my peers for living in language with me. To Zach and Emma for their friendship, and to Emma for creating the toad and cover of my dreams. Thank you to my parents for their love and unquestioned belief in me. To Little Max (2007–2020), my dog angel, who kept me company as I wrote these poems and stayed as long as he could. To Fernando, *por vida*.

Jonno Rattman

TAISIA KITAISKAIA was born in Russia and raised in America. She is the author of *Ask Baba Yaga: Otherworldly Advice for Everyday Troubles* and its follow-up, *Poetic Remedies for Troubled Times from Ask Baba Yaga*, as well as *Literary Witches: A Celebration of Magical Women Writers*, a collaboration with artist Katy Horan and an NPR Best Book of 2017. She has received fellowships from Yaddo and the James A. Michener Center for Writers. She lives in Austin, Texas.

PARTNERS

ADDITIONAL DONORS, CONT'D

Danielle Dubrow
Denae Richards
Dori Boone-Costantino
Ed Nawotka
Elizabeth Gillette
Elizabeth Van Vleck
Erin Kubatzky
Ester & Matt Harrison
Grace Kenney
Hillary Richards
JJ Italiano
Jeremy Hughes
John Darnielle
Jonathan Legg
Julie Janicke Muhsmann
Kelly Falconer
Kevin Richardson
Laura Thomson
Lea Courington
Lee Haber
Leigh Ann Pike
Lowell Frye
Maaza Mengiste

Mark Haber
Mary Cline
Max Richie
Maynard Thomson
Michael Reklis
Mike Soto
Mokhtar Ramadan
Nikki & Dennis Gibson
Patrick Kukucka
Patrick Kutcher
Rev. Elizabeth & Neil Moseley
Richard Meyer
Sam Simon
Sherry Perry
Skander Halim
Sydneyann Binion
Stephen Harding
Stephen Williamson
Susan Carp
Theater Jones
Tim Perttula
Tony Thomson

SUBSCRIBERS

Audrey Golosky
Ben Fountain
Ben Nichols
Carol Trimmer
Caroline West
Charles Dee Mitchell
Charlie Wilcox
Chris Mullikin
Chris Sweet
Courtney Sheedy
Dan Pope
Daniel Kushner
Derek Maine
Elisabeth Cook
Fred Griffin
Heath Dollar
Hillary Richards
Ian Robinson
Jason Linden
Jody Sims
Joe Milazzo
John Winkelman
Kate Ivey

Kenneth McClain
Kirsten Hanson
Lance Stack
Lisa Balabanlilar
Luke Bassett
Margaret Terwey
Martha Gifford
Megan Coker
Michael Binkley
Michael Elliott
Michael Lighty
Molly Bassett
Molly Lunn
Nathan Dize
Neal Chuang
Radhika Sharma
Ryan Todd
Shelby Vincent
Stephanie Barr
Ted Goff
Vincent Granata
William Pate

AVAILABLE NOW FROM DEEP VELLUM

MICHÈLE AUDIN · *One Hundred Twenty-One Days*
translated by Christiana Hills · FRANCE

BAE SUAH · *Recitation*
translated by Deborah Smith · SOUTH KOREA

EDUARDO BERTI · *The Imagined Land*
translated by Charlotte Coombe · ARGENTINA

CARMEN BOULLOSA · *Texas: The Great Theft* · *Before* · *Heavens on Earth*
translated by Samantha Schnee · Peter Bush · Shelby Vincent · MEXICO

LEILA S. CHUDORI · *Home*
translated by John H. McGlynn · INDONESIA

SARAH CLEAVE, ed. · *Banthology: Stories from Banned Nations* ·
IRAN, IRAQ, LIBYA, SOMALIA, SUDAN, SYRIA & YEMEN

ANANDA DEVI · *Eve Out of Her Ruins*
translated by Jeffrey Zuckerman · MAURITIUS

ALISA GANIEVA · *Bride and Groom* · *The Mountain and the Wall*
translated by Carol Apollonio · RUSSIA

ANNE GARRÉTA · *Sphinx* · *Not One Day*
translated by Emma Ramadan · FRANCE

JÓN GNARR · *The Indian* · *The Pirate* · *The Outlaw*
translated by Lytton Smith · ICELAND

GOETHE · *The Golden Goblet: Selected Poems*
translated by Zsuzsanna Ozsváth and Frederick Turner · GERMANY

NOEMI JAFFE · *What Are the Blind Men Dreaming?*
translated by Julia Sanches & Ellen Elias-Bursac · BRAZIL

CLAUDIA SALAZAR JIMÉNEZ · *Blood of the Dawn*
translated by Elizabeth Bryer · PERU

JUNG YOUNG MOON · *Seven Samurai Swept Away in a River* · *Vaseline Buddha*
translated by Yewon Jung · SOUTH KOREA

FOWZIA KARIMI · *Above Us the Milky Way: An Illuminated Alphabet* · USA

KIM YIDEUM · *Blood Sisters*
translated by Ji yoon Lee · SOUTH KOREA

JOSEFINE KLOUGART · *Of Darkness*
translated by Martin Aitken · DENMARK

YANICK LAHENS · *Moonbath*
translated by Emily Gogolak · HAITI

FOUAD LAROUI · *The Curious Case of Dassoukine's Trousers*
translated by Emma Ramadan · MOROCCO

MARIA GABRIELA LLANSOL · *The Geography of Rebels Trilogy: The Book of Communities;*
The Remaining Life; In the House of July & August
translated by Audrey Young · PORTUGAL

PABLO MARTÍN SÁNCHEZ · *The Anarchist Who Shared My Name*
translated by Jeff Diteman · SPAIN

DOROTA MASŁOWSKA · *Honey, I Killed the Cats*
translated by Benjamin Paloff · POLAND

BRICE MATTHIEUSSENT· *Revenge of the Translator*
translated by Emma Ramadan · FRANCE

LINA MERUANE · *Seeing Red*
translated by Megan McDowell · CHILE

VALÉRIE MRÉJEN · *Black Forest*
translated by Katie Shireen Assef · FRANCE

FISTON MWANZA MUJILA · *Tram 83*
translated by Roland Glasser · DEMOCRATIC REPUBLIC OF CONGO

ILJA LEONARD PFEIJFFER · *La Superba*
translated by Michele Hutchison · NETHERLANDS

RICARDO PIGLIA · *Target in the Night*
translated by Sergio Waisman · ARGENTINA

SERGIO PITOL · *The Art of Flight* · *The Journey* ·
The Magician of Vienna · *Mephisto's Waltz: Selected Short Stories*
translated by George Henson · MEXICO

EDUARDO RABASA · *A Zero-Sum Game*
translated by Christina MacSweeney · MEXICO

ZAHIA RAHMANI · *"Muslim": A Novel*
translated by Matthew Reeck · FRANCE/ALGERIA

C.F. RAMUZ · *Jean-Luc Persecuted*
translated by Olivia Baes · SWITZERLAND

JUAN RULFO · *The Golden Cockerel & Other Writings*
translated by Douglas J. Weatherford · MEXICO

TATIANA RYCKMAN · *The Ancestry of Objects* · USA

JESSICA SCHIEFAUER · *Girls Lost*
translated by Saskia Vogel · SWEDEN

OLEG SENTSOV · *Life Went On Anyway*
translated by Uilleam Blacker · UKRAINE

MIKHAIL SHISHKIN · *Calligraphy Lesson: The Collected Stories*
translated by Marian Schwartz, Leo Shtutin,
Mariya Bashkatova, Sylvia Maizell · RUSSIA

ÓFEIGUR SIGURÐSSON · *Öræfi: The Wasteland*
translated by Lytton Smith · ICELAND

MIKE SOTO · *A Grave Is Given Supper: Poems* · USA

MÄRTA TIKKANEN · *The Love Story of the Century*
translated by Stina Katchadourian · SWEDEN

FORTHCOMING FROM DEEP VELLUM

AMANG · *Raised by Wolves*
translated by Steve Bradbury · TAIWAN

MARIO BELLATIN · *Mrs. Murakami's Garden*
translated by Heather Cleary · MEXICO

MAGDA CARNECI · *FEM*
translated by Sean Cotter · ROMANIA

MIRCEA CĂRTĂRESCU · *Solenoid*
translated by Sean Cotter · ROMANIA

MATHILDE CLARK · *Lone Star*
translated by Martin Aitken · DENMARK

LOGEN CURE · *Welcome to Midland: Poems* · USA

PETER DIMOCK · *Daybook from Sheep Meadow* · USA

CLAUDIA ULLOA DONOSO · *Little Bird*, translated by Lily Meyer · PERU/NORWAY

LEYLÂ ERBIL · *A Strange Woman*
translated by Nermin Menemencioğlu · TURKEY

ROSS FARRAR · *Ross Sings Cheree & the Animated Dark: Poems* · USA

FERNANDA GARCIA LAU · *Out of the Cage*
translated by Will Vanderhyden · ARGENTINA

ANNE GARRÉTA · *In/concrete*
translated by Emma Ramadan · FRANCE

GOETHE · *Faust, Part One*
translated by Zsuzsanna Ozsváth and Frederick Turner · GERMANY

PERGENTINO JOSÉ · *Red Ants: Stories*
translated by Tom Bunstead and the author · MEXICO

JUNG YOUNG MOON · *Arriving in a Thick Fog*
translated by Mah Eunji and Jeffrey Karvonen · SOUTH KOREA

TAISIA KITAISKAIA · *The Nightgown & Other Poems* · USA

DMITRY LIPSKEROV · *The Tool and the Butterflies*
translated by Reilly Costigan-Humes & Isaac Stackhouse Wheeler · RUSSIA

FISTON MWANZA MUJILA · *The Villain's Dance*, translated by Roland Glasser · *The River in the Belly: Selected Poems*, translated by Bret Maney · DEMOCRATIC REPUBLIC OF CONGO

GORAN PETROVIĆ · *At the Lucky Hand, aka The Sixty-Nine Drawers*
translated by Peter Agnone · SERBIA

LUDMILLA PETRUSHEVSKAYA · *Kidnapped: A Crime Story*, translated by Marian Schwartz · *The New Adventures of Helen: Magical Tales*, translated by Jane Bugaeva · RUSSIA

JULIE POOLE · *Bright Specimen: Poems from the Texas Herbarium* · USA

MANON STEFAN ROS · *The Blue Book of Nebo* · WALES

ETHAN RUTHERFORD · *Farthest South & Other Stories* · USA

MUSTAFA STITOU · *Two Half Faces*
translated by David Colmer · NETHERLANDS

BOB TRAMMELL · *The Origins of the Avant-Garde in Dallas & Other Stories* · USA

CPSIA information can be obtained
at www.ICGtesting.com
Printed in the USA
JSHW081124250123
36802JS00005B/8